Leadership in the Trenches:
Developing Front-line Leaders

Penny D. Miller, SPHR, SHRM-SCP

Copyright 2018

Penny Miller

All rights reserved. No part of this publication may be reproduced, distributed, or transmitted in any form or by any means, including photocopying, recording, or other electronic or mechanical methods, without the prior written permission of the publisher, except in case of brief quotations embodied in reviews and certain other non-commercial uses permitted by copyright law.

ISBN-13: 978-1725127937

ISBN-10: 1725127938

DEDICATION

To the finest front-line leaders, the noncommissioned officers of the armed forces, for their dedication to our country, their service, and their leadership of the men and women who serve our country around the world.

To all of the under-appreciated first line supervisors who make the wheels of business turn.

ACKNOWLEDGEMENTS

Many thanks to my Beta readers for their suggestions on making this book better: Don Swift, Stuart Langley, and Jeri Moore.

And a special thanks to Peggy Browning of Browning Books for her handholding during the publishing process.

Table of Contents

Introduction	2
Trust: The Foundation	4
Why Supervisors Are So Important	9
Moving From Peer to Supervisor	16
The Competencies	21
Compliance	27
Customer Service	32
Process Excellence	37
Coaching	42
Setting Expectations/Goals	46
The Power of Feedback	53
Ask Questions	57
The Art of Delegation	60
Rewards and Recognition	64
Expertise/Continuous Learning	68
Communication	73
Collaboration and Teamwork	78
Conflict	83
Change	87
Hire Right!	91
Summary	94
For More Information	95
About the Author	96

Foreword

Those who haven't been in the American armed forces may not be familiar with the expression "in the trenches."

It refers to World War I trench warfare and is used to mean "on the front lines" or "where the work really gets done."

Introduction

In my earlier book, *Winning the War for Profit: Developing Leaders Where It Really Matters*, I make the case for the critical importance of frontline supervisors. I don't want to recreate that book here.

However, a brief recap of a few important points is appropriate. Approximately 40% of newly promoted managers are no longer in their jobs 18 months later (Manchester Consulting, Inc.) They have either been fired, quit, or returned to their previous position. Clearly, this is disruptive to the supervisor, the work center, and the company.

Winning the War for Profit was focused on businesses—why supervisors are important and how to select, train and support them.

This book picks up where *Winning the War for Profit* leaves off. The focus of this book is on the skills supervisors need to be effective in their jobs. The focus is the supervisor and is intended to be used to better prepare supervisors for success. Therefore, the book talks to the supervisor.

If you're a supervisor, and your company doesn't provide supervisor training, you can use this book to gain some understanding of your role and the skills needed for success.

If you're a company trying to create or improve your supervisor training, this book can provide a framework and supplemental material for your program.

This book is not intended to be the be all and end all on developing first line leaders. It is intended to introduce you to the things you need to know to be successful. Entire books have been written about each of the subjects in this book. Instead, I've provided you a bite-size bit of knowledge, some of my school-of-hard-knocks lessons learned, and a platform to begin moving yourself forward in each area.

Each chapter in this book is structured as follows:

- A few questions to think about why the chapter is important and where you as a supervisor stand on the subject to be discussed.
- The meat of the chapter with information on the topic.
- Suggestions for activities to improve your skills.
- Summary of key points.

The material in this book mirrors similar lessons in The Supervisor Academy online courses.

For more information about The Supervisor Academy, email thesupervisoracademy@gmail.com. *(Mention this book in your email and get a code for one free course!)* To see all of the courses available, go to https://supervisor-academy.thinkific.com/. Courses are being added, so check back periodically.

Chapter 1

Trust, the Foundation

"Trust is the glue of life. It's the most essential ingredient in effective communication. It's the foundational principle that holds all relationships."
– Stephen Covey

- Do you believe you are trustworthy? Why?
- Do your managers, peers, and reports believe you are trustworthy?
- Think about your best supervisors. Did you trust them? What did they do to make you feel that way?
- Think about your worst supervisors. Did you trust them? What did they do to make you feel that way?

Before we go any further, let's talk trust.

The fundamental issue that underlies most of a supervisor's success is trust. It is the foundation of everything else. This is the one attribute that <u>must</u> be in the character of a supervisor. In this case, it doesn't matter if you feel you are trustworthy. It matters that others think you are.

In some of my training classes, I have participants list the attributes of the person they consider to be the best supervisor they ever had; then we discuss the worst supervisor. Everything the participants mention falls on one side of the question of trust or the other.

If I do not trust my supervisor, I will not take risks. I will not bring problems to his attention. I will be careful about following his instructions. I am constantly in cover-my-ass (CYA) mode.

If your people can trust you, they will work for you. They will also be more likely to accept change and to support unpopular decisions.

A Case in Point

To illustrate this, let me take an example from my own experience. I wanted to volunteer my workplace for the test of a new organizational structure. I knew absolutely it would be disruptive. It would be uncomfortable in terms of culture. It would be complicated. And I was certain the people who worked for me would hate the idea. However, I also felt it was an important change for the long-term success of the organization.

I sat down with my managers and explained what I wanted to do and asked for their opinions. No surprise…..they hated it. They voiced the arguments I had thought about in the days preceding our meeting. I asked them to think it over and try to look at the good of the organization in the long run and to get back to me about whether they could support the test because it would not work without them and the people who worked for them.

Some hours later, my deputy came in and said they had talked about the test. They still hated the idea because it was going to be hard, disruptive and a huge cultural change. Then he said, "We trust you. We know you would not have made this decision unless you thought it for the best. We will do everything possible to make it work."

They did. It worked.

The Concept of a Trust Bank

Stephen Covey talks about a trust savings account in his book *The 7 Habits of Highly Effective People*. He talks about how our everyday actions either make deposits into our trust account or withdrawals. Any guess which tend to be bigger?

Think about it. If you had a person do something you felt was dishonest, underhanded, or backstabbing, how likely are you to trust that person again? How long would it take for them to regain your trust?

Our actions tell people whether we are trustworthy. Small withdrawals add up over time. Are you dependable? Do you keep your word? Do you value your employees?

Some things seem very small, but they are part of the impression people have of you. For example, I have a person I work with I really like and overall, I consider him to be a trustworthy person, except when it comes to time. He will frequently be late. I have to build in extra time, knowing I likely will have to wait for him. This is not a huge deal, balanced against all of the other good traits he has, but it is irksome.

However, let's talk about a previous boss of mine. There were a number of ways he showed he wasn't trustworthy, but the one that truly nailed it for me was when he modified a chart in a presentation I put together for him to lead the business owners to a false conclusion. I addressed the issue to him after the meeting, and he thought it amusing he could get them to support his position without telling them a direct lie.

Most of us are between these two examples. If I tell a person I will get back to her by the end of the day, do I? If one of my people comes up with a better way of doing things, do I make sure they get the credit? If Joe and James are both late, do I take corrective action with both, or only one of them?

We've all heard it: "Actions speak louder than words."

The Importance of Values

A person of integrity acts in accordance with her values. It is important to understand what values a company and a leader not only espouse, but what values they live by.

I got caught in this once. I was conducting interviews with references for a potential hire for a top-level management position for a company. The people I talked to mentioned how much integrity the person had. This came up multiple times.

When it was all said and done, the gentleman was hired, and it was one of the worst hires I was ever involved with. I didn't ask the crucial question: what values were important to this person? It is true that he operated in accordance with his values. Unfortunately, the only value he truly had was his personal self-interest, not the good of his employees, the customers, or the organization.

Don't assume your personal values and the values of the organization line up. Check. Then be sure those values truly govern decisions and actions. It is one thing to say, "Employees are our greatest asset." It is another to treat them like that. Don't assume everyone understands values the same way. They don't.

An organization should use values as the primary yardstick to determine a person's suitability for a leadership role. They should use values to measure success.

A supervisor should constantly think about how her actions exemplify her personal values and those of her organization. Do her actions indicate she is trustworthy or not?

Put Your Knowledge to Work

For the next two weeks, at the end of the day, review how you built (or destroyed) trust by your actions. Consciously make an effort to make a deposit to your trust account every day.

At the end of the two weeks, review your progress. Do you have more deposits than withdrawals? Did you improve over the two weeks?

I know a senior leader that does this every single day and has for years. He is widely viewed as a very trustworthy person. It isn't an accident.

Key Takeaway

If you aren't seen as trustworthy, you aren't supervisory material. Period.

Chapter 2

Why Supervisors Are So Important

"A good boss makes his men think they have more ability than they have so they consistently do better work than they thought they could." –
Charles Erwin Wilson

- Who represents the company in the minds of your customers?
- Who is responsible for hiring, training, and directing the work of those customer-facing people?

Businesses have to make money. This includes non-profit businesses. Nonprofits can't provide their services without the money to do so. In the best of all worlds, the business will make enough money to give its employees a decent paycheck and to reinvest in the business.

That being the case, I would argue there is no better place to invest dollars than first-line supervisors.

Not every business owner gets this. At one of my previous places of employment, the owners decided they needed to save on payroll. We had a very flat organizational structure. One of the owners asked me, "Why don't we get rid of all of the supervisors? They get paid a lot, and they don't really do anything." At that time, we had around 350 employees, 8 first line supervisors, 3 senior managers and 53 owners. Knowing the owner as I did, I just said, "So, you're okay talking to your receptionist yourself if you are unhappy with her performance?" To which, the reply was, "No, I don't want to deal with that."

Jobs saved.

But first-line supervisors are so much more important that just keeping those higher up the chain from having to deal with unpleasant conversations with employees.

Most leadership studies focus on the people at the top of the organizational ladder. Those people are important, but any of us who have been anywhere near the top know that it doesn't matter what grand vision we have, if the people in the organization do not support you in the day-to-day actions necessary to convert your vision into reality, it will never happen.

The people who are key to success in an organization are the front-line supervisors. Leaders at all levels are important, but organizations that truly want to thrive need to focus on that very first step of the leadership ladder. But that bottom rung is the leadership rung most ignored.

Before we go any further, let's talk about employee engagement. You may have heard this term already, but you may not know what it means. It is an important concept.

Employees knows that there is a minimum amount and quality of work that will allow them to keep their jobs. If that is the case, why do more than that? In most cases, they won't earn more money. It is just more work. This is where employee engagement comes in. Employee engagement is that discretionary effort employees give to the organization that they don't have to. They choose to.

You have about 10% of your employees who will work hard no matter what. You have about 10% of your employees who will have to be let go because they aren't going to work, no matter what you do. That leaves 80% in the middle.

This 80% will range from just barely satisfactory performance to just a tiny bit below your very best. The goal is to shift the performance of all employees up by getting them engaged with their work. Even a small shift upwards can have a major impact on results. Not everyone has to move into that top 10% to make a difference.

A Tale of Two Supervisors

I had a work center that was floundering badly. Internal audits showed that the work coming from that work center was neither accurate nor timely. The individuals in that work center were working hard, to include a lot of overtime, but they weren't making progress. The employees were frustrated, even though they liked their supervisor. They were tired of the overtime, the customer complaints, and their coworkers in other departments belittling them because of their poor-quality work.

The supervisor argued that the problems were caused by a lack of manpower. I gave him additional staffing, but the situation didn't improve. I decided to change the supervisor. It wasn't a popular decision—as I said, the employees in that work center did like the supervisor as he had a friendly, outgoing personality.

The supervisor I moved into the section ran a tight ship. He set high performance standards and enforced them. Just as importantly, he invested a lot of time in training his employees (the previous supervisor "didn't have time" to train his people.)

Within 90 days, the audit rosters were cleaned up, the backlog of work was gone, the extra staffing was released back to other requirements and there was no more overtime. The employees didn't like the new supervisor initially (in fact, "didn't like" is probably a little mild for their feelings) but they respected him a lot by the end of the first month and wanted to keep him by the end of the 90 days.

Same workload, same people, same equipment and supplies. The only change I made was the supervisor. This story can be replicated time and again.

Regardless of the scientific findings, this story and dozens like it, illustrate why the supervisor is so important. But let's review some of the recent findings anyway.

I am going to focus for a moment on a report from Harvard Business Review called, *Frontline Managers: Are They Given the Leadership Tools to Succeed?* In a survey, senior management said that frontline managers are important to achieving business priorities.

Between 70% and 80% agreed that frontline managers were very important in:

- Achieving a high level of customer service
- Helping the organization achieve business goals
- Achieving high productivity
- Achieving high employee engagement
- Contributing to effective communication

But when asked how proficient their supervisors were at various skills they considered important, they agreed the answer was "not so much." Citing only two specific competencies, only 33% felt their frontline managers were proficient at business-based decision making. Only 20% were proficient at developing talent.

Ninety-two percent of these same senior managers believed a frontline manager's lack of leadership development negatively impacts employee engagement and 79% believed the lack of leadership development moderately or negatively impacts the organization's performance.

Given all of this, these same leaders invest heavily in choosing and developing these frontline leaders, right? This is where the behavior and logic break down. It makes you wonder about the business-based decision making of our senior managers. Only 19% of companies felt their supervisor training was average to excellent and only 12% felt they invest enough in training. Why is that?

Company leadership admits that supervisors are very important for mission-critical functions. They admit that our supervisors lack the skills to be successful in those tasks. But then the same leaders admit their companies are not investing enough in training. You have to ask the question, "Why?" There are basically two reasons.

First, a lack of development dollars because of focus on profitability. Training dollars are one of the first dollars cut when financial resources are tight. Training is considered a "nice to have" instead of a "necessary to have." This behavior occurs in opposition to studies which have shown that companies that maintain their training in the face of recession do better during the recession and come out of the economic downturn in great position to capitalize on the economic recovery.

Our focus on short-term earnings negatively impact our long-term success.

Secondly, companies rely upon the trickle-down model for leadership development. In other words, higher level managers get development first, with the expectation that knowledge will "trickle down" to lower level managers. This theory of leadership development works about as well as the trickle down economic theory.

Here are just a few other reasons companies need to focus on supervisors:

- The right managers contribute <u>48% more profit</u> than average managers. (Source: *Frontline Managers*)
- Managers account for at least 70% of the variance in employee engagement scores across business units. (Source: *Why Great Managers Are So Rare*)
- Businesses say that manager and supervisor involvement was "extremely important" or "very important" to the success of their change efforts. (Source: *Prosci's 2009 Best Practices in Change Management* benchmarking report)
- Total return to shareholders (TRS) over a 3-year period is 186% higher for those companies with a high level of employee trust versus those with a low level of trust (Source: Watson Wyatt)
- Ninety-three percent of employees rated their relationship with their immediate supervisor as "very important" or "important" to their job satisfaction (Source: SHRM Research Survey)

If you are still stuck on the first bullet, you should be. That statement, by itself, should justify every penny of investment organizations make in their supervisors.

Put Your Knowledge to Work

Your work is critical to your company's success. Act like it. Use the information in this book to help your employees perform better than they thought they could.

Pick one thing. Just one. Focus on improving that one area. Once you are more comfortable in that area, pick the next one.

Key Takeaway

There is a complete disconnect between the value of supervisors and the investment decisions related to their development. For supervisors, this means you have to take responsibility for your development.

Chapter 3

Moving From Peer to Supervisor

"A manager is not a person who can do the work better than his men; he is a person who can get his men to do the work better than he can." – Frederick W. Smith

- Before you became a supervisor, what did you think the job entailed?
- How does the job differ from what you envisioned?
- What is hard for you?
- What do you enjoy most about the job?
- What is your biggest headache?

Although I began my work life as a supervisor, most people move into a supervisory position from a front-line worker position. This has some advantages. The supervisor knows the work. In fact, the new supervisor is often chosen because he is very good at the job. Unfortunately, there are also very real problems with moving from the front line to supervisor.

Most people who are promoted into their first management positions have unrealistic expectations of the job. As a front-line worker, our perception of the supervisor's job is not very realistic. Many feel the supervisor's only job is to tell other people what to do, but it is much more complex. It is often a rude awakening to find what comes along with being the boss.

Probably the thing that comes as one of the biggest shocks is that the boss isn't really the boss.

Almost all of us have people above us, and we're caught between them and the people we supervise. Some days it seems as if we can't make anyone happy.

There are many stressors about moving into a supervisory position for the first time. The lack of preparation means we are unprepared for the realities of the job. I often assign the article, "Becoming the Boss" by Linda Hill as a reading assignment for my leadership development program. It usually elicits some good discussions about what people expected the job of first-line supervisor to entail versus the reality.

We'll discuss three of the bigger hurdles to being successful at the job.

- The supervisor's job is no longer only about the technical aspects of the job.
- It can be difficult for the new supervisor to move into an unfamiliar role when it is so easy to fall back into the familiar.
- The friend and coworker relationship with fellow workers can interfere with some of the tough calls supervisors have to make.

The Supervisor's Job is No Longer Only About the Technical Aspects of the Job

When your leadership team chooses you to be a supervisor because of your technical expertise, they usually feel an expert in the task will ensure the work is done correctly. However, your job is no longer just about getting the technical tasks done, it is about getting others to get them done—an entirely different skill set.

Although technical competence is important for first-line supervisors, you don't have to be the most competent in terms of doing the job. Instead, other skills better predict success—not just for the supervisor, but for the work center they will oversee.

These skills include emotional intelligence, the ability to develop and maintain professional relationships, the ability to communicate, your adaptability to change and the ability to train, coach and develop others.

It's Difficult to Move into an Unfamiliar Role

The role of supervisor is distinctly different than that of a line worker. The work is not only more complex and less concrete, but there are new skills to learn and a lot of pressure managing multiple priorities.

Many new supervisors get so frustrated by the unfamiliar demands that they fall back into the comfort of the familiar. Although many small companies may need a "working supervisor", many supervisors spend more time on routine technical tasks because it is comfortable for them. It's what they know they can do well. Consequently, they don't always spend the time on their supervisory tasks—they aren't sure what they are or how to do them, leading to avoidance.

Supervisors who are highly technically competent have an even more difficult time allowing others to do the work (i.e., to delegate.) They feel surrendering the work to others who are less skilled will lead to lower quality. This is because their focus is still on the work task, not supervisory tasks, like developing others.

This is the organization's fault. Organizations should outline expectations, prepare people for the job, and coach them to success. Most don't.

Friend and Coworker Relationships Can Interfere With Tough Calls

The move from friend to boss is a hard one. As a worker, we tend to have an "us" vs. "them" mentality. Suddenly, with the promotion to supervisor, we have become a "them." Our relationships with fellow employees are important and provide a lot of satisfaction, but then those relationships change. The dynamics of the relationship change and often, we aren't prepared for it.

I am not one to say there can be no personal relationship between a supervisor and the people they supervise, but there does need to be a line. Some people can handle a fuzzy line; some need a solid demarcation. Supervisors are responsible for upholding the organization's values and objectives. Sometimes this means your employees are not going to like the decisions made. Others will try to take advantage of you, relying on their personal relationship with you to bend (or break) the rules.

Establishing a support system with other supervisors is a big help. Those that have been through the experience can provide a listening ear and advice.

Put Your Knowledge to Work

What are you struggling with in terms of your supervisory role? Ask for help. Attend training, find a mentor, read.

Examine your work relationships with your former coworkers to see if those relationships have changed with the change in position. If those relationships are obstructing your success, it's time to have a frank discussion with those people to make clear how your new relationship will work.

Talk to some other supervisors you respect (they don't have to be in your company) to get their insight and suggestions on how to make the transition easier.

Key Takeaway

Making the transition from worker to supervisor is hard and made harder through lack of preparation for the role.

Chapter 4

The Competencies

"The leader's job is not to do the work for others, it's to help others figure out how to do the work for themselves, to get things done, and to succeed beyond what they thought possible." – Simon Sinek

- Look around you at the people you see that you consider to be great first-line supervisors—what is it that makes them that way?
- What do they spend their time "doing?"

I mentioned in the last chapter that the skill set that got you the promotion to supervisor is not that same skill set that will make you successful now that you are here. So, what are important competencies for supervisors to have?

By the way, "competency" is one of those HR buzzwords you're going to hear on occasion, but what does it mean? A competency is basically a combination of knowledge skill, and personal attributes that the organization feels are necessary for a person to be successful in a given role. It provides a basis for measuring success.

Some core competencies for first line supervisors include:

- Communication
- Collaboration
- Customer service
- Expertise/Continuous learning

- Process excellence
- Coaching (Staff development)

We'll be getting into these competencies later, so for now, let me just give you a general summary of what is included in each area.

Communication

If I had to choose the most important communication skill, it would be listening. If you think back to the best/worst supervisor exercise in "Trust, the Foundation," people would describe the best supervisors by saying, "She really listened to me when I needed to discuss a problem." Conversely, the worst supervisor "didn't want to hear any ideas or problems."

Although many new supervisors worry about standing in front of a group and giving a presentation, most supervisors do few presentations beyond a tool box meeting. There is nothing formal about that and most seem comfortable speaking in that environment. In most organizations, first-line supervisors do not give many (if any) formal presentations.

First-line supervisors need to be able to talk to people one-on-one. It is more your ability to relate, to ask questions and to listen that make the real difference between success and failure. It isn't necessary that you be glib and polished in your speech. It is necessary for you to be clear about what you want. It is critical to be someone who can engage your brain before opening your mouth. Easier said than done.

I tend to avoid putting people who are easy to anger into supervisory positions—they tend to say and do things that get them and the organization in trouble. However, this can be overcome, if the person recognizes this is a fault and is willing to work at it.

The ability to write does seem to begin to trip up many people when they become supervisors. Most front-line employees have little need to write beyond filling out forms and writing some email. Supervisors often write reports, performance appraisals, disciplinary actions, work instructions, and email. These documents matter.

However, you can learn to write. New supervisors need to understand that poor spelling and grammar affects your credibility up the chain and what you put into writing is a record you may have to answer to in any investigations, government inquiries or lawsuits.

Customer Service

By customer, I mean anyone who uses a work center's product or service. That doesn't have to mean the same person who buys your company's products and services. Everyone on your company's team needs to be focused on that external customer, but for many work centers, their focus is on supporting the overall effort by providing support to other internal departments.

This is another area where there is a big change from front-line worker to supervisor. Many new supervisors have trouble broadening their focus from their individual job to the success of the entire enterprise. When I start my leadership development program for new supervisors, one of the key behaviors many companies want to see change is "being able to see the big picture."

This can be coached, but you have to be willing to discuss changes to processes, most especially those that have an impact on your work. If you are willing to change how you do things to improve how the work center operates, then you are likely to carry that mindset into a larger role.

Expertise/Continuous Learning

One of the things front-line employees want is for their supervisor to be a resource for them—a person to go to with questions and problems. When I went into the Air Force, the NCO that was charged with training me said I needed to learn everyone's job and be able to do their jobs as well or better than they. I devoted myself to that, but later decided that is a little overboard.

Yes, I do need to know what they do. I do need to know enough to be a resource. But I have since developed the belief that if I have to do everyone's job, why do I need them? I may need to be able to pinch hit in a workload crunch or when someone is absent. But more importantly, I need to know how to get the tools, equipment, money, and supplies my people need. I need to facilitate the flow of information between sections. I need to know where to go to get answers. If I don't know something, I need to know who does or where to go to get the answer. That's what I need to know. I need to be an expert at <u>my</u> job, not their job.

From an organizational point of view, I need supervisors with a broader, more systems view toward their jobs. I also need people who won't let their expertise get out of date. I want my supervisors to be reading, talking to others, and learning new technology and processes. I want them to learn from others and to pass that learning on. I want them to be good teachers. I need them to value and reward good ideas, even those they didn't come with and perhaps don't agree with.

Process Excellence

Although this may sound like I am contradicting myself, I'm not. I am not talking about a supervisor able to do the job herself, but having a focus on high quality, timely, and efficient work. In addition, I want her to be looking for new, better ways of doing the work all of the time. Whether they themselves come up with creative, innovative ideas or improve and pass on the ideas of the people who work for them, I never want to hear, "If it isn't broke, why fix it?"

Coaching (Staff Development)

The primary role of every supervisor is to grow and develop the people who work for them. I often ask the supervisors I coach, "Who could take your place if you don't make it to work tomorrow?" The answer is almost always, "No one." In some cases, they may say their lead could keep the production process moving for a while, but the other supervisory tasks would not get done. When I hear that, my response is, "Then you're not doing your job."

It does happen that you may have a small work center in which no one currently there wants the supervisor's job. That's okay. I don't want to promote someone into a position they do not want, but if that is the case, I need to look elsewhere in my company for talent that may be able to make a move or be prepared to go outside the company for a replacement when the time comes. And I have to prepare the people in my work center to be able to get by without me for a time until the company can determine who my replacement will be.

One of the statements that makes me insane is, "I don't have time to train." We have time to fire and rehire. We have time to redo work. We have time to deal with customer complaints. But we don't have time to train. The sound you hear is my head exploding. We'll talk more about this later in the book.

One key aspect of training is cross training. Not only should each person know their job, there should be at least one other person who can do the job (even if not as well) for every position. There is no excuse for a customer to need assistance or to have an order that needs to go out and the process is at a standstill because someone is on vacation. None.

Put Your Knowledge to Work

Keep track of where you spend your day. You can probably get a clear picture of where you spend your time within a week. Is it task-oriented or people-oriented? Although you may need to spend some time doing daily work tasks, really think about what you are doing and why. Are you spending enough time doing your job or are you spending too much time doing the work you've hired others to do? If you are doing the work, what is everyone else doing?

Decide what supervisory tasks you are not completing or completing as well as you should because you don't feel you have time. Make time to do those tasks and teach others how to do the day-to-day work, so you don't have to.

Key Takeaway

As a supervisor, your job is helping others do their jobs well. You are a facilitator, a trainer, and a problem-solver. That is your value to the organization.

Chapter 5

Compliance

"Let's make it simple: Government control means uniformity, regulation, fees, inspection, and yes, compliance." ~ Tom Graves

- Do you know your company's policies (rules?)
- What types of situations mean you need to get outside help (your HR department, for example)?
- Have you found yourself "on the carpet" for violating some law or regulation you didn't know existed?

Nobody likes compliance. It's boring. It's a lot of work. But in many cases, it keeps us, our employees and our customers safe. Regardless of whether we like it or not, we have to do it. Compliance is built around habits. What you measure and enforce, gets done. What you don't, doesn't. It really is that simple.

This is an area where reminders matter. Checklists, templates, and other aids help people remember everything that has to be done and can be set up so that the employee has to affirm they completed each step.

When I was responsible for supervisor training in a previous place of employment, I put new supervisors through an initial training, primarily focused on compliance. Each month, we had a supervisor's meeting, which focused on some training and discussion on some issue where supervisors could share their ideas and experiences. Looking back at that, it wasn't nearly enough, although it was more than most organizations have and as much as I could get ownership to sign on to.

When a company anoints you as a supervisor, the company is responsible for the things you say and do in the performance of your job. This is a key reason companies should be careful when selecting their supervisors. Every supervisor should receive training before they become a supervisor and on a regular basis thereafter. Training and development should be targeted to the needs of the supervisor.

For supervisors, you should be aware that although your company has liability for your words and actions, it doesn't mean you do not. Many laws have civil, and in some cases, criminal, penalties that can be applied to you.

Compliance

Compliance is probably the area companies do best in training their supervisors. The types of training included in this area are those mandated by law or regulation as well as training relating to reducing the risk associated with the supervisor's role.

Compliance is fairly mechanical. You either are or you are not in compliance with laws, regulations and policies.

Compliance is purely an effort to control risk. Companies hope that by providing this training, supervisors will not do things that garner complaints to regulatory agencies or land them in court.

Compliance training is not a "one and done" item. Many compliance items don't come up often, so supervisors need regular reminders of specific areas of concern. Laws, regulations and policies also change—regular, updated training needs to be done to be sure supervisors are current in their knowledge. If your company is not providing this training to you, you need to look for options to get it for yourself.

I am not a fan of more is better when it comes to compliance training. Companies often err in training by giving the supervisor more information than she needs. You are not the HR professional nor the company lawyer. You need information that applies to you and the types of situations you will run into in their day-to-day work. And then, you need to know who to call if you encounter a situation outside the norm.

At the very minimum, supervisors should have some training in:

- **Ethics**. I start with this one. I know many companies do not make a concerted effort in this area, but as employees tend to follow the ethical practices they see, not the practices written in the company's code of conduct, you need to thoroughly understand your company code of conduct and your role in modeling the appropriate behaviors. You are the person your employees see every day. You have to know an ethical issue when you see it and know what to do.
- **Equal Employment Opportunity/Sexual Harassment**. Most companies make this entirely too long. You need to know what the policy says, what type of behavior is not acceptable and what to do/not do if someone comes to you with a complaint. You need to understand what retaliation is. It doesn't take hours to do this. In fact, I find that the longer the training is, the less supervisors remember. I can do this training in 20 minutes. It covers what they need to know, without a bunch of fluff to obscure the message.

- **Fair Labor Standards Act (FLSA.)** This is the single largest area of employment law liability for a company. You need to understand your company's policies on pay (I am assuming your company policies comply with the statute.) The focus should be on the items that most closely affect you. For example, "Yes, we must pay people for all time worked—regardless of where or when that work takes place." Therefore, supervisors absolutely cannot request nor allow people to work off the clock.
- **Other Employment Laws that Apply to Your Company.** You wouldn't need training on Family Medical Leave if your company is not a covered employer. But if you are a covered employer, what do you need to know? You need to have a good idea when FMLA may apply and when people are eligible—just enough knowledge to know when to refer the employee to the person who administers the program for a detailed analysis and to get details about the administrative requirements. You need to know how to account for the time. And you need to understand about retaliation. That's it. Let HR handle the details—that's what they get paid for.
- **Company Policies.** Have you read, and understand, your employee handbook? You are the one who will be getting the complaints and the questions about policies, so you need to have accurate information about the policy and why it is important. Do you have the current handbook? Make sure.
- **Discipline and Termination.** This is part of company policies, but I separate them out because there is more involved than just knowing company policies about discipline. There is a certain level of skill here. The goal of discipline is to change behavior, so it is not just a

matter of knowing the administrative details of applying discipline but learning how to discuss discipline with the employee to be sure the employee can take the correction to heart. By the time we get to termination, we aren't looking to change behavior, but how we go about terminating employees can make a big difference in possible complaints or lawsuits later, our company's reputation with our workforce and in the community, as well as the likelihood of violent behavior.

Put Your Knowledge to Work

If your company has a handbook, find the most current version and study it. Granted, it's not exciting reading, but it's important. Make a list of questions and visit HR to get them answered.

Find out if your company has supervisor training. If not, suggest it, even if it is in the form of a lunch and learn. Look for professional development courses and ask to attend.

If all else fails, find training resources and do it yourself. The website http://supervisor-academy.thinkific.com/is a place to start.

Key Takeaway

Yes, your company should ensure you have the compliance training you need to keep them, and you, out of trouble, but it doesn't always happen. Ask.

If your company doesn't provide this training, find it yourself.

Chapter 6

Customer Service

"Customer service should not be a department. It should be the entire company." ~ Tony Hsieh

- How do you feel about your customers? Are they inconvenient?
- Is the customer always right?
- What do your customers want most?
- How do you know if your customer is getting what they want/need?

Our jobs would be easy without having to deal with customers, right? Perhaps, but we wouldn't have a job without customers. They come with the territory.

Just to be clear, when I talk about customers, yes, I am talking about the people and companies who actually purchase our goods and services. However, let's not forget the other departments and coworkers who need things from us in order to satisfy those who are purchasing. We'll talk about our internal customers when we get to the chapter, Collaboration. In this chapter, we're going to stick to our external customers.

Believe me, I know customers can be difficult. They're demanding, sometimes unreasonable, and occasionally rude. But since our business cannot survive without them, our plan is to keep them happy.

I listened to another speaker talk about customer service at a conference I attended. She said customer service is easy. You need to:

- Know what the customer wants
- Know how the customer wants it
- Give them what they want the way they want it

Peter Shankman has written a couple of books about customer service and speaks to business conferences about the topic. He says, "Most customer service is crap. If you're just a little better than crap, your customers will love you."

I get what they're saying and to some extent, agree. But I like to go a little further.

Yes, we do need to know what our customers want. We know what we believe they should want, but our thoughts and theirs are not always the same. We need to be asking all the time.

Yes, we need to know how our customers want to receive our goods and services. Times change. Our customers are changing. Serving them the way we have always done will lead us down the path to extinction. People want mobile services and access 24/7 to information. One size doesn't fit all—you have to figure out what YOUR customers want and how they want to receive it.

- My son won't buy from any business without a website presence
- I won't deal with a company that greets me with a voice mail tree when I call, unless I cannot find an alternative
- I've moved my business over $1
- All of us have some business that we never returned to because of some customer service issue

In one respect, I disagree with both of the people I mention above. Our goal should be to Wow! people with our customer service. What that means depends upon our industry, our product or service, and the market segment we are trying to appeal to.

I am going to use experience with a couple of doctor's offices as a way to illustrate my point.

Doctor's offices are not considered a place you look at for good customer service, although they should be. Good customer service tells patients they are important and are more than the disease they have or the check they are going to write. Patients who feel as if the doctor and her staff care about them are much less likely to sue if something doesn't go right. But when you talk to patients, they are usually not too happy. Exorbitant wait times is the primary complaint, but there are many others.

I have one specialist I see who always runs on time. Always. The advantage is that when you have an appointment, you know you're going to get in, get seen, and be on your way. I like that. I can plan my day. I don't have to block out my entire day from work for a 20-minute appointment. The downside for some is that if you are late, the doctor won't see you, because he is not going to keep the next patient waiting. I'm fine with that; I still operate under the military rule on timeliness—if you're not 15 minutes early, you're late.

I was once referred to an oncologist because some test results looked like I might have cancer. Needless to say, this is a stressful time in any person's life. This was one of the absolute best doctor visits I have ever had. The doctor and his staff obviously thought about how their patients were feeling and went out of their way to reduce the stress.

I was seen on time.

My husband and I were not taken to a sterile and unattractive exam room to start with. Instead, we were taken to a small meeting room, painted in calming colors and furnished with comfortable furniture. We were given something to drink.

The doctor came in immediately and sat down at the table with us. He immediately said, "I've looked at all of the test results, and I don't believe what you have is cancer. You definitely have a problem and the only way to be absolutely sure you don't have cancer is to do surgery, but here's what I think is going on."

Then he went through the test results. He explained in plain English what the results meant. He recommended the next step. He answered our questions. His folks scheduled the surgery before we left. I had clear and concise directions for everything I needed to do between that appointment and surgery.

Later that evening the nurse called me to make sure I didn't have any questions or concerns that occurred to me after the visit. Someone called me a couple of days before the surgery to remind me of what I needed to do and to ask again if I had any questions. The surgery went well...the doctor's part at least. I didn't have the same level of customer service from the hospital, but that's another story.

What am I saying? It would have been more efficient for the doctor and his staff to do things a different way, but it wouldn't have been as effective. I would have been okay with the same level of service I have come to expect from doctor's offices, but I wouldn't be talking experience as an example of how to treat people 15 years later.

We're often told the customer is always right. That's not always true. Some customers are not worth the amount of stress and work they cause. Some will never be happy. Some will try to cheat you—and some will succeed. Some will be rude. Some will disrupt your business and prevent other customers from having a good experience. That doesn't excuse unprofessional behavior on your part or the part of your employees, but neither should your employees have to put up with bad behavior.

In the end, the people who determine whether your customers are happy are your employees. They make the product correctly or they don't. They get things done on time, or they don't. They are cheerful and professional, or they're not.

As a supervisor, your job is to give them the training and the tools to provide excellent customer service. Your job is to make sure they know what your expectations are about what behaviors constitute good customer service and enforce those behaviors. Your job is to model the behavior you want.

Put Your Knowledge to Work

Sit down and think about your customers and what they want. Think about what could make their experience with your company not just good, but great. What behaviors can move the needle to make that happen? Make a list. Set expectations. Follow up. Don't know what your customers like/don't like about your customer service? Ask them!

Key Takeaway

There's a difference between good customer service and a positive experience the customer will rave to others about. Your employees make that difference.

Chapter 7

Process Excellence

"I don't want to assume our tradition of excellence is a guarantee of future excellence." – Dave Heineman

- How do you measure results in your area?
- How do your results compare to industry standards? Best practice? Do you know?

Supervisors are under a lot of pressure to deliver results. That is the bottom line measure of our effectiveness. Product shipped on time. Dollar value of sales. If you hit your performance targets this quarter, you're likely to be asked to meet higher targets next quarter.

Do more with less. Sound familiar?

When companies send their supervisors to me for leadership development, one of the areas of concern is often that the supervisor doesn't seem to be looking for better ways of doing things. Companies want to see processes produce quality outputs, faster, cheaper, and more safely. And yes, I do know that at some point, you don't get more with less—you get less with less. But in many organizations, that is not the issue yet.

Supervisors often feel employees want to do the minimum amount of work. Certainly, that's possible. When employees aren't engaged, they aren't interested in giving extra effort above that required to stay employed.

However, if we can get employees engaged, then high performance standards are motivating to employees. When I ask employees to tell me about their best supervisors, the comments <u>always</u> made include statements like: "He had high expectations and held people accountable." "She pushed us hard." These same comments are not made when I ask about their worst supervisors. In fact, employees are likely to say, "He didn't care."

But to push for excellence means we have to know what excellence is. What is the level of expected performance in your company? How do you know? What do other organizations like yours do against that standard? Who is best in class and what standards are they hitting?

You may say, I don't have enough people. Our budget keeps us from buying the supplies and equipment we need. We don't have time to look for better ways of doing things; it is all we can do to get the product/service out the door in the time we have.

It doesn't always take more people, a bigger budget, or newer equipment to kick ass.

One of the first people I supervised was Sergeant Harris. It was 1979. Military budgets were not very large at that time. In fact, I remember bringing office supplies (and toilet paper) from home, because we didn't always have enough on hand. This was before computers. We had one electronic typewriter in the work center—you could type in one sentence on a very small screen and look at it to see if it was correct. Print that sentence and do the next. That was the high-tech equipment.

Sergeant Harris had a manual typewriter. A very old manual typewriter. The carriage was held on with a rubber band

and if you hit the return lever with too much force, that carriage would fly across the room.

All correspondence was done in multiple copies with carbon paper and the NCO in charge (NCOIC) of the work center was a stickler for accuracy. If he could see any evidence of correction, whether on the original or one of the carbons, he tore up the document and you started over.

That meant your work had to be perfect.

Sergeant Harris had a broken-down manual typewriter and was trying to meet the expectation for perfection in his work. He took great pride in the fact that the NCOIC rarely found a mistake in his work.

You're probably thinking, "I take pride in my work. The problem is all of these people who work for me."

Let's move forward a few years. I was working for the base commander and one day he came into the office and told me he had fired one of the branch chiefs because of an unsatisfactory audit. He asked me to move to that branch and get it straightened out.

I admit, I wasn't excited at the prospect. I had managed a similar organization before and wanted a different challenge. But from a leadership perspective, turning around a poor performing work area is something I love to do.

I went over to my new workplace and needless to say, morale was in the cellar. The people knew their audit results were unsatisfactory, and they felt guilty that their boss was fired.

In less than six months, we received a new audit, and the base commander was told our current programs were excellent in every area.

What happened? Same people. Same facilities. Same budget, equipment and supplies. Basically, we stopped focusing on what we didn't have and decided to make the best of what we did.

For example, the organization had a large vehicle fleet. Every quarter, there was a competition with an award for the outstanding vehicle and vehicle manager. Usually, one of the new vehicles won that competition.

I had a young airman who was in charge of the one vehicle we had--the oldest panel van in the fleet with a lot of miles on it. The competition was based upon cleanliness, preventive maintenance, and paperwork.

My young airman felt he didn't have a chance at that award with an old vehicle. But we made winning that award a performance goal and compared his scores with the scores of the vehicles that won, so we could track his progress and compare his scores to the best in the fleet. It took a few quarters, but he won. The best maintained vehicle on the base.

That old van shined like it just left the showroom. And so did he.

People want to win. It's that simple.

We just need to be sure we set the standard, give them feedback on their performance against that standard, and provide adequate tools. We didn't spend any more money. He made the difference with elbow grease and meticulous attention to detail.

I just helped him to believe the goal was possible.

Put Your Knowledge to Work

You know the performance standard you have to meet to keep your bosses happy. That doesn't mean you have to settle for that. Find out what others are doing. If you don't have contacts in jobs like yours, read industry magazines or ask higher management what those standards are. Make these higher standards into goals.

Key Takeaway

People want to win. Winning feels good.

It's that simple.

Chapter 8

Coaching

"Because a thing seems difficult for you, do not think it impossible for anyone to accomplish." – Marcus Aurelius

- Think about a person who helped you be better. It could be a teacher, family member, or boss. What did they do that helped you become better?
- Think about a person who discouraged you or put obstacles in your way to performing better. What did they do?

Companies want supervisors to develop the people who work for them but don't help them learn and develop the crucial art of coaching.

Coaching is improving performance. Coaching requires the coach to focus on each person's strengths. We tend to focus on our employees' shortcomings. If you see only what people do wrong, you will not excel at developing high performance.

There are a number of subsets of skills required to do a good job of coaching: goal setting, feedback, questioning, delegation, etc. The best way for supervisors to learn to coach is to have the behavior modeled by those above them, but as we have said before, that often doesn't happen.

Trust is a vital component of coaching—on both sides of the coaching relationship.

Coaching is all about improving performance by focusing on specific skills needed to achieve success. Generally, there is someone who acts as a coach to help the person being coached evaluate their current performance, determine their strengths, set goals and provide feedback.

In order to be successful, coaching requires two things. First is a trusting relationship between the coach and the person being coached. The second is a focus on the person's strengths.

Coach from a Place of Strength

Most of us focus on what our employees do poorly, not what they do well. I don't do everything well and neither do you. We overcome our weak areas by capitalizing on our strengths.

Let's use my sister as an example.

She played on very competitive softball teams when she was younger. The problem was, she was slow. Not a little slow—turtle slow. If she was on third base when a batter hit the ball, they might just push her over home plate. That slow.

Often a coach will focus on how slow a player is at running bases. But for most of us, it takes a lot more effort to improve something we are bad at than something we already do well.

A coach might decide that a person who cannot run the bases couldn't play on one of these competitive teams. But that wasn't the case. Because there were other things she did extremely well.

She was the catcher. I won't say catchers don't move, but they don't move much. They guard the plate. They have to catch well, and they have to be able to throw accurately and quickly anywhere on the field. They have to understand strategy.

In my sister's case, she could do these things and she could bat. She batted in fourth position most of the time. Because she was slow, unless the coach told her otherwise, she was aiming for the fence. Every time.

Instead of worrying about her very slow base running, the coach focused on all of the other skills that made her a valuable part of the overall team success. That's what we should be focused on when we are coaching to improve performance.

Yes, if a person has a fatal flaw, we have to address it. But if we can work around it by enhancing other skills, it's a win.

In order to coach employees, I have to think about it. I can coach haphazardly, but I won't be as successful.

I get paid to coach people to be better leaders. I have to discover their strengths and weakness. I need to figure out how they look at the world and what's important to them. Then I have to come up with a plan to help them achieve their (and their company's) goals. There is nothing haphazard about it.

You need to do the same with each of your employees. You don't really have to set aside large blocks of time to coach. It can easily be done in small increments of time—discussing goals and expectations, giving them feedback on performance, asking questions about their work, recognizing good work, suggesting other ways of doing things, etc.

None of these take a lot of time—we just need to make some time on a regular basis and do it.

Coaching Tool Kit

There are a variety of ways to coach people and you need to use them all at different times. I call this my coaching tool kit. I don't want a long chapter, so we're going to break the coaching tool kit apart and address many of the tools in separate chapters.

The tools in that tool kit involve: goal setting, feedback, questioning, and delegation. We'll be talking about these tools in the following chapters.

Keep in mind that the same technique won't work for every person. Each person has their own goals, and each has a different priority about what's important. We need to discover what works with each person. If a technique isn't working, try something else.

Put Your Knowledge to Work

Think about each of your employees. What is it they do well? They must do something right or you would have fired them by now. Can you think of a way to strengthen their strong points to compensate for their less awesome talents? Sit down and make a plan on how you are going to help each person perform better.

Key Takeaway

Coaching your employees to improved performance is the most important job you have. Make time for it.

Chapter 9

Setting Expectations (Goals)

"The trouble with not having a goal, is that you can spend your life running up and down the field and never score." ~ Bill Copeland

- Do you know your company's goals?
- Do you know your department's role in achieving them?
- Do your people know their part?

Before we can coach a person to high levels of performance, we (and they) have to know what's expected. People cannot hit a target that doesn't exist.

I have had managers get upset because an employee asks for goals. Why? "Nobody gave me goals."

If a new employee asks me about goals, I am doing the happy dance. (I say new employee, because the rest have goals.) That tells me they <u>want</u> to do well and give me what I want.

However, many supervisors stink at setting goals. For example, "Improve customer service." What does that mean?

What you think it means and what your employee thinks it means are likely to be two different things. How will you know when you have it?

Setting SMART Goals

You've probably heard about what's referred to as a SMART goal. You'll find a couple of different versions of what the various letters mean, but they're all close.

You'll be more successful at explaining, evaluating and meeting goals if you follow this process for defining goals.

I am going to use a very simple goal to illustrate the SMART goal process.

Let's say it is January 1 and you decide to make a goal for the year. (Yes, I know most people scoff at New Year's resolutions, but that's because they don't treat them like goals—a soapbox for another day.)

A common goal is: I am going to lose weight this year.

The morning of December 31 you jump on the scale. You still weigh what you did on January 1! But you wanted to lose weight!

You skip breakfast and eat almost nothing all day. You go to the gym and do a long workout. You hit the scale again before bed and you weigh ¼ pound less than you did on January 1. Hurray!

You made your goal!

Didn't you?

You lost weight. But is that what you were thinking on January 1?

Probably not.

Let's revisit our New Year's resolution and turn it into a SMART goal. We're going to compare it to the customer service goal we mentioned earlier.

SMART is an acronym for:

- **S**pecific
- **M**easurable
- **A**ttainable
- **R**elevant
- **T**imebound

Goal: Improve customer service

Is it Specific?

No, what constitutes customer service? What does it look like?

Is it Measurable?

Maybe. If I knew what constituted customer service, I could probably figure out a way to measure it. But as stated, I have no clue what it is or how to measure it, so how do I know if I do it?

Is it Attainable?

Probably, but how to I reach something that I don't know what it is?

Is it Relevant?

Conceptually, yes. Who doesn't want better customer service? After all, we want to keep our customers happy. But it's all a matter of faith.

Is it Timebound?

Well, no. I didn't say this was a New Year's goal, so I cannot assume it is to be done by the end of the year. This could be a never-ending quest, since I will never know if I have arrived.

Goal: To lose 20 pounds by December 31

Is it Specific?

Twenty pounds is twenty pounds. You make it, or you don't.

Is it Measurable?

The scale doesn't lie (if you don't tamper with it.)

Is it Attainable?

Maybe. It depends upon your weight/body mass. In my case, since I have gained 65 lbs. since I left the Air Force, losing 20 lbs. should be doable.

What if I said I wanted to lose 100 lbs.? This might be attainable, but not likely. And my brain will know it.

If we (or one of our employees) see a goal as non-attainable, the goal isn't motivational.

No one wants to feel as if they are being set up for failure. If I don't try, I can't fail.

We may know a goal is reachable because of past experience, but our people may not. If performance is poor, an intermediate goal can be challenging.

Once our work center makes the intermediate goal, the higher goal seems possible.

Is it Relevant?

In other words, why should they care about this goal? In this case, I don't care—that's why it isn't a goal for me.

Just like our kids, "Because I said so" isn't going to illicit more than a token effort. Sometimes employees feel like their company management pulls goals out of the ether. If this is a truly important thing to accomplish, we should be able to articulate why they should care.

Is it Timebound?

Yes. This needs to be done by the end of the year. However, with a date that far out, it is easy to lose track and then discover around Thanksgiving time that we have 20 (or 25) pounds to go. So intermediate timelines can help use stay focused and on track.

Yes, my goal is to lose twenty pounds by the end of the year. To do that, I will love five pounds the first quarter, five pounds the second, five pounds the third, and five pounds the fourth.

This keeps me focused on the goal and gives me an early indication that the goal is in danger of being unmet, so I can make a course correction earlier than later.

Setting Performance Standards (Expectations)

Let's switch from goals to performance standards before we move on. We often assume "everyone knows" what acceptable standards are, and they don't. We need to be clear about our expectations. What do you mean by "on time" to work? What is "clean?" What you mean and what the employee thinks you mean are often different. Be clear. Show and tell is not a bad thing. Tell the employee how to get the "A."

Let's look at an example. I had a fast food manager who was upset. "My people have no work ethic." I asked him what he meant. "I tell them to stock the front. They tell me it's done. I go out to the front and it isn't stocked. They're just lazy." (For those wondering, "the front" is the sidebar in the restaurant with the condiments and paper/plastic products you use to eat.)

Think about it. Who are often the people who work at fast food restaurants? Many times, they are young people in their first job. They need a flexible schedule. Well, I raised a couple of these people, and I can tell you, if I told them to stock the front and they went out and saw a single ketchup packet, then you have ketchup.

I told him to stock the front the way he wants to see it. Then take his employees out and tell them, "When I tell you to stock the front, this is what it should look like when you are done." Then go item by item and explain the standard for success—I call it "How to get an A."

When we set performance standards, we are usually too fuzzy. Our employees need to know exactly what we want.

Our standards need to be consistent. If we set a standard, it's the standard. It isn't different for one person versus another. It isn't different when I am in a good mood than it is when I'm not. People should not have to wonder if the same work is going to result in a different grade.

Goals are motivating, used correctly. As I said in an earlier chapter, people like to win. Goals are a way to keep score. Make goals challenging—your people will enjoy meeting the challenge.

Now that we have a goal or a performance standard we need accountability. In other words, we need to compare our performance against the standard (or goal).

This is what we mean by feedback, which is the topic for the next chapter. Feedback is the next step in accountability.

Putting Your Knowledge to Work

Look at your department goals. Are they SMART? If not, restate them so they are.

Are your performance standards crystal clear? If there could be any confusion, try again. Show and tell is a good way to demonstrate.

Key Takeaway

Tell your people how to get the A.

Chapter 10

The Power of Feedback

"When we make progress and get better at something, it is inherently motivating. In order for people to make progress, they have to get feedback and information on how they're doing." ~ Dan Pink

- Do you know how your bosses view your performance? Are you achieving the results they want? Are your priorities the same as theirs?
- What about your employees? Do they know how they are doing in your eyes?

Feedback is nothing more than telling someone how their performance compares to a standard. We all need feedback. People want feedback. The vast majority of our people want to do well and make us happy. They just don't know how.

There is no other tool that can turn performance around faster than feedback. None.

Providing feedback is done properly, which is normally not the case.

Most of us do a poor job of giving feedback. Generally, it is because we weren't taught how. Our bosses probably stink at it too. Sometimes we worry about hurting feelings and don't want to deal with the drama or the conflict that comes with bad news.

The bottom line is that none of us can improve without feedback. Denying a person the opportunity to improve their performance is just wrong.

There are two types of feedback: positive and negative. Both types of feedback are necessary. Use positive feedback to get more of what you want. Use negative feedback to stop behavior you don't.

We don't give positive feedback enough. I know how important it is, and I don't give it enough. I hire people to do a good job, so when they do a good job, I don't reinforce it with positive feedback. After all, that's what I hired them for. That is just wrong. Everyone likes to hear they are doing well.

We tend to be overly general when giving positive feedback. "Great job!" If I am your employee, that gives me a warm fuzzy. I'm happy that you're happy. I don't really know exactly what I did that made you happy, but I feel good.

Just because I feel good doesn't mean I will do that same thing again, because I don't know what I did. If we want people to repeat a behavior, they have to know exactly what behavior I want. Compare "Good job on that report, John." To "Good job on that report, John. It was clear, concise, and well organized. It was obvious you did your homework and I can feel confident in following your recommendation."

Is John going to make sure to be equally concerned about ensuring future reports meet this same level of clarity in the future? Absolutely. The first pat on the back made him feel good, but if that is the only feedback John gets, he may over time, be less careful, especially if he has many things to get done. Until he gets to the point where you tell him you are unhappy. Now he knows the minimum level of performance.

I don't want the minimum.

Managers tend to give mostly negative feedback. But again, we tend to do a poor job of it. We let things go until we just can't stand it any more and then we tend to give negative feedback in an overly emotional way. The person gets defensive because they feel like they are being attacked.

Other times managers don't want to confront the issue directly, so in a staff meeting they will say, "We need to pay more attention to XYZ. Some of us are not paying attention to detail and we've had too many parts rejected in quality control." Everybody in the room knows that John is the "some of us." Except John. He thinks he is doing OK.

Let's talk about how to do feedback correctly. There is a simple format.

Be specific. What exactly is the employee doing right or wrong? Give a specific example. How does that compare to the standard?

Be impersonal. This is not about the person. It is about the behavior/performance. Supervisors say things like, "You have a bad attitude." "You don't have work ethic." "You're lazy." No. Stick to the behavior. This is the performance you've given, and this is what I expect.

Make it timely. Give your feedback as soon as possible after the event. The more time there is between the event and the feedback, the more likely it is your memory of what happened and your employee's memory of what happened will differ. However, if you are angry, walk away and talk about it later. Nothing good comes from opening your mouth when you are mad.

Why is this important? Employees often feel like the things we get excited about are not worth it. If we have set a standard, there must be a reason for it. Why do you care? Why should they?

Check for understanding. And no, I don't mean for you to ask, "Do you understand?" The question sounds like you think they are stupid. The only answer you'll hear is "Yes."

Gain commitment. This is especially true for negative feedback. I want to hear them take responsibility for change.

Positive feedback if the fastest way to change behavior. This is a catch-them-being-good process. If you are trying to get a behavior you don't currently see, praise anything close. You'll draw them to what you want. For example, if you are trying to get people to show more initiative, then if they do anything without you telling them, praise it, and be sure to use the word, "initiative."

You should be giving at least three (yes, 3) positive feedbacks for every negative. For most of us, it's the reverse.

Put Your Knowledge to Work

For the next few weeks, focus on giving feedback, using the formula outlined in this chapter. Look for reasons to give positive feedback. Is there a behavior you want to see more of? Look for opportunities to praise that behavior.

Key Takeaway

People cannot improve without feedback. If we don't give it, we are cheating our employees.

Chapter 11

Ask Questions

"The art and science of asking questions is the source of all knowledge." ~ Thomas Berger

- Does it seem like your employees ask you questions they should know the answer to?
- Do they ask the same questions over and over?

It is a common complaint from supervisors that their employees repeatedly ask questions they should know the answer to. Yes, they do. Because you're an enabler.

We are often promoted to a supervisory position because we are good at our jobs. We know how things are done. We see ourselves as a resource to help our people. When they have questions, we answer them. It's expedient. That's what we're there for, right?

Yes. And no.

Remember the Tale of Two Supervisors I talked about at the beginning of this book? The primary tool the second supervisor used to turn around the performance in his area was asking questions. Not answering questions.

The first supervisor was the resource. His people asked, and he answered. But if he wasn't available to answer, nothing got done, because they weren't sure what to do.

For your employees, asking questions is safe. If they ask you what to do, you tell them, and they do it. It is not their fault if something goes wrong.

But this creates dependency and it brings down performance.

We should be teaching our people how to think. How to exercise judgement. How to be independent. We do that by asking questions.

Jane comes in with a problem and asks you what to do. Instead of telling her, ask a question like, "What do you recommend?" You might get, "I don't know." Turn her around and tell her, "Think it over and come back with an idea, and we'll talk it over."

She may come back with the perfect answer, in which case some positive feedback is in order, "I knew you had the knowledge to figure this out. It makes me feel good that I can count on you to come up with solid solutions."

She may come back with a totally harebrained solution. In that case, more questions are in order. "Lead me through your reasoning—how did you decide this was the best option?" If there are factors she didn't consider, "What about this fact? Will your solution work in this case?" If she didn't consider something, "Where would you get this information?"

Helping our people be independent improves performance, makes them feel empowered, and gives you more time to focus on your other responsibilities.

I can hear you thinking, "This takes too much time. It's easier to give them the answer so we can get back to work."

Yes, it does take more time in the beginning, but it will pay off later.

Obviously, if the situation is urgent and must be dealt with immediately, give them the answer. You can come back to it later to discuss it.

Put Your Knowledge to Work

Resist the temptation to make life easy by answering your employee's questions. Use the opportunity to train your people in how to solve problems for themselves. Over the next several weeks look for opportunities to ask questions instead of answering them.

Key Takeaway

Don't be an enabler. Teach your people to be independent.

Chapter 12

The Art of Delegation

"If you want to work 160 hours a week, don't delegate. But you are going to crash and burn." ~ John Baldoni

- Do you feel comfortable delegating to your people? Why/Why not?

Failing to delegate is one of the primary reasons new supervisors fail. You cannot do everything you are tasked to do if you do not delegate.

Delegation is giving someone else the authority to do a task.

Why is it that so many of us have problems delegating? Because we can delegate the authority, but we are still responsible for the outcome. If the task isn't don't correctly, we have to answer for it.

Sometimes we feel guilty as if we are making work for one of our employees.

There are good reasons to delegate. As mentioned above, delegation frees up some of your time to focus on other tasks.

Another reason is that it is motivational. Employees know there is a level of trust that goes into delegation, and they feel good that you have that trust in them.

Delegation can improve the productivity of your department by ensuring others can do things in your absence.

Delegation is a good training tool, especially for those you think may be candidates to move into your job someday.

Delegation is not dumping. I have been dumped on a lot. People do feel frustrated and angry in those cases. I used to have a boss who would put things in my chair when I went to the restroom or to lunch. I would come back to find papers in my chair. No explanation. No information. Just a pile of paper.

Obviously, I was supposed to do something with it. Sometimes it was obvious. Other times, not. I would have to hunt him down to get the information I needed to get the job done. I don't know why he couldn't save us both time by talking to me.

Delegation is risky—for us and for the employee. We are worried about the job getting done right and the employee is worried about the consequences if it isn't done right. Having a process to delegate correctly can help both the supervisor and the employee get a good outcome.

Delegation Process

Step 1. Decide what task to delegate. Some things should not be delegated.

Those things that come with being a supervisor: discipline, performance discussions, etc., should never be delegated to someone else.

Your boss may have asked for you to handle something yourself due to confidentiality. If so, do it yourself.

Step 2. Decide who to delegate to. Is it because you think they have a unique skill set to do it? Because you want them to learn a specific task to help the work center function better or to prepare them for additional responsibilities?

Step 3. Talk to the person and explain the task. Tell them why you are assigning the task to them, what specific outcome you are looking for, how you will evaluate their performance, and the timeline for completing the task.

Check for understanding.

Step 4. Set progress reports. If the person has done the task before and you are confident in the person's ability to do the task and get it done on time, you may not need this. For everyone else, set timelines to check in.

If it is the first time I have given the employee the task or if the task is complex, I am probably going to meet within a week. "Go ahead and look over this project. We'll get together on (date) so I can answer any additional questions you have."

This expressly says you expect questions. It ensures the person gets started on the task and doesn't put it off. It also lets you feel confident they are not going off in the wrong direction. Regular checkpoints keep the person moving and allows you to make course corrections early.

Step 5. Let them do the task. When you give a person a task, tell them the outcome you want and the timeline. Let them decide how to get it done. If you are going to tell them step-by-step what to do, you might as well do it yourself.

Step 6. Give feedback. When the task is finished, let the person know how they did—both good and bad.

By following this process, you greatly increase the likelihood you will get the job done correctly and on time. That will make both you and your employee feel better.

Putting Your Knowledge to Work

Decide on a task to delegate. Decide who. Follow the delegation process. Evaluate your success after the task is complete.

Key Takeaway

Delegation isn't dumping. It is a critical tool to improve performance.

Chapter 13

Rewards and Recognition

"People may take a job for more money, but they often leave it for more recognition." ~ Bob Nelson

- What recognition programs does your company make available for you to recognize your employees?
- Do your employees like your company's rewards and recognition programs?
- Do your employees feel like they are recognized for their accomplishments? How do you know?

Supervisors aren't usually in a place to decide how companies reward their people—compensation, benefits, and incentives. But you need to understand what's available and what criteria the company uses to assign the appropriate rewards, so you can use the system to help you attract and keep the best people.

You may not have a lot of say in the big picture of the design of rewards in your company, but you have a lot of say in recognition. Your company may have recognition programs, but you are the person who determines who is nominated for these programs. And you have total control over the recognition that means the most.

This is one area where it is obvious that one size does not fit all. What one person really wants and will work hard for can be a great disincentive for another.

We had an employee of the quarter program. Each supervisor could nominate one person. There was a selection process, a portion of which included an interview with a panel of managers who talked to the employees about their job and the reasons they were nominated.

We had one employee who was nominated. She deserved to be. She was by far and away the best performer in her section. Everyone knew it. After she came out of the interview, she came to see me and told me she would not go through the process again. She said, "I appreciate that my supervisor wants to recognize me for doing a good job, but I won't do this again. I was up all night stressed about this interview, and I felt like I was going to throw up. I hate it. I am going to be sure I am not nominated again. I am going to throttle back. I don't want to do that, because I want to do a good job, but I'm not going through this again."

I went to see her supervisor and told him we needed to find another way to recognize his employee because this particular recognition program was a disincentive for her. The supervisor then had to decide how he was going to handle future nominations. Did he send no one if none of his employees could out do her performance or did he send the second best, when everyone would know they weren't the best performer in the section? It's a tough decision to make.

Several years ago, I learned an important lesson. Companies operate under the assumption that recognition has to cost a lot of money. I did a survey of the people who worked in my department about what type of recognition the employees would value. We didn't have a lot of money to spend and the company policies put some restrictions on what we could do.

You know what answer came back? The employees wanted someone to give them a personal thank you for a job well done. That's it. I created some business card-sized cards. When I found out one of my people did something worth recognition, I wrote a sentence or two on the back about what that was. Then I walked into their work center and told them thank you in front of everyone.

I left that job many years ago. I happened to be in that organization a few years ago and one of the employees I presented one of those cards to about a decade before asked me to come to his work area. He had plaques and certificates all over his wall. But tacked to a surface directly in front of his keyboard was that card. He said it was the most meaningful award he ever received.

Employees want to know we recognize they're important. Their jobs mean something, and they make a difference. They love cash awards and trinkets and paid time off. All of these are important. But the most important thing is for someone to say thank you. It costs you nothing.

Recognition works best when the recognition is matched to what is important to the person and when the employee can see a clear connection between performance and the reward or recognition given.

Another consideration is the recognition of the person versus the recognition of the group. Personally, I lean more to team rewards, but some combination of team and individual is important. Too much focus on individual rewards can lead to internal competition that can be destructive to the team environment.

The correct balance depends upon what type of work environment you are trying to foster.

Put Your Knowledge to Work

Find out how your company structures its rewards and recognition programs and how much flexibility you have. If you haven't taken the time to recognize the work of your people, do it now.

Key Takeaway

One size does not fit all. What is important to each of your people and how can you use that knowledge to help them want to perform at a higher level?

Chapter 14

Expertise/Continuous Learning

There are no secrets to success. It is the result of preparation, hard work and learning from failure. ~Colin Powell

- How do you keep up with changes in your trade or profession?
- How do you keep up with changes in company policies and processes?
- How do you encourage learning in others?
- How do you react to failure and mistakes? Do you have a process to learn from them?

Being the best today doesn't mean you will be the best tomorrow. Nothing stays the same, no matter what the job.

There are always new techniques and technology. Laws and regulations change. Companies evolve. Society's and workers' expectations of the workplace continue to change.

We have to work to ensure we stay current in those area important to our jobs. A significant part of our job is to be a resource to our people and an expert advisor to our bosses. Neither of those is a sure thing if we allow our knowledge to become dated.

I would like to think every organization has a process to prepare people for their roles as a supervisor. I would also like to see them help supervisors learn and keep current on all of the skills needed to manage people and on company policies and procedures.

However, I also realize this is not the case in every company. That means you have to do it yourself. Take charge of your learning.

If you are not learning, you will eventually become obsolete. You will not have the respect of your employees, your peers, or your bosses.

You should be looking for opportunities to learn new things. Build a network of people who do the same sort of work you do. Talk to others to get their insight and expertise. Read industry publications.

Take classes. There are a lot of online classes, some of which are free and some of which are relatively inexpensive. Your local community college should have pertinent continuing education courses. Seminars and conferences are more expensive, but often have a variety of workshops that you would not otherwise find locally.

Your company should be willing to invest in your education, but don't be surprised to find they are not. If they are not, that means it is up to you.

You also need to invest in the learning in your work center. Again, your company may not be able to or be willing to invest in training and education. But there is no reason not to do it yourself.

Here are some ideas;

- Cross-training. There is no reason only one person knows how to do something—including you. You should have at least two people who can do a task. One may be much better at it than the other, but both should be able to get the job done.

- Continuity documents. Some sort of documentation should exist in the work center for every job that would help a new person get up to speed quickly or help a person who has never been trained at least figure out where to start. Checklists, templates, flowcharts, and contact information can be a lifesaver. This documentation is a pain to put together the first time but is not difficult to keep current.
- On-the-job training. Most companies stink at on-the-job training. It is haphazard at best, highly dependent upon the person doing the training. A plan is a huge help. It doesn't have to be complicated, but there needs to be one. What does everyone in your work center need to know? What tasks does the person in each job need to know how to do? Are you sure they know how to do them correctly? How?
- Training sessions. Every work center should have some sort of regular training. It doesn't have to be long, but it needs to be regular. If training is done all of the time, learning and sharing knowledge becomes an expectation. Five minutes to discuss a safety topic or some change in a process. Twenty minutes to teach everyone a new procedure. You don't have to do all of the training, and in fact, you shouldn't. Get others involved.
- Encourage questions. "Why?" is the best question in the world. It teaches people to think. It exposes unnecessary steps and policies. It helps make procedures relevant.
- Failure analysis. Most companies treat mistakes as a sin. No one likes mistakes. They cost time, money, and are embarrassing. Since they cost a lot of money, it doesn't

make any sense not to capitalize on your investment, so this next section talks about this.

I don't like to make mistakes. No one does. I can remember early in my career, I really messed up. I was embarrassed and knew it was going to be a problem for my work center and my boss. I was not looking forward to confessing.

I went in to my boss and told him what I had done. He asked, "How did this happen?" "How are you going to fix it?" "What should you have done?" "How are you going to ensure this doesn't happen again?"

Then he said, "Look, you're going to make mistakes. The only way to avoid mistakes is to do nothing. You need to learn from them. But you shouldn't make the same mistake again."

How to deal with a mistake?

Recognize it. Acknowledge it. Learn from it. Fix it. Move on.

This is one thing I learned from the military. Examine everything.

What went well? What worked? What didn't? Is there anything we could have done differently that would have improved the result?

Do this even when you don't think a mistake was made. It gets people in the habit of looking for better ways of doing things.

It sends a message that we are always learning. And it gets people to acknowledge and accept responsibility for errors.

We have a tendency to throw people under the bus when they make a mistake.

This means people play it safe. They don't try new things. They don't take responsibility.

It leads to finger pointing, blame games, and dishonesty.

Put Your Knowledge to Work

Create a learning plan. In what area could you improve your expertise? Pick one thing that if you knew more about would make you better at your job and develop a plan to learn about it. Once you've made the plan, execute the plan.

Key Takeaway

Take every opportunity to learn. Mistakes happen. Learn from them and move on.

Chapter 15

Communication

The art of communication is the language of leadership. ~ James Humes

- What are your strengths and weaknesses as a communicator?
- Have you had times when you wondered if you and your employees were speaking the same language?

It should come as no surprise that one of the areas that I spend a lot of time in my supervisor coaching practice is communication. It isn't always what a supervisor says that causes a problem, but the way she says it.

Communication is such an all-encompassing topic, it can be intimidating. Although there are many areas in communication, there are certain key areas that are vitally important to first-line supervisors.

A critical item for communication is the message. If you cannot state the message you want people to remember in one clear, concise sentence, the likelihood is that the message will get lost between you and the person you are trying to communicate with.

You need to understand who you are talking to. There are dozens of things that can go wrong and cause misunderstanding. It's a wonder we ever get it right. Who are you talking to? What do they know about the subject of the message you're sending? How are they going to feel about it?

All of these can affect how you decide to communicate your message.

The most needed (and most lacking) communication skill is listening. Most of us think we are good listeners. We are not. When I ask employees if their supervisor is a good listener, most say no.

Supervisors think they can multi-task. Study after study has shown this not to be the case, but even if we can, we shouldn't. When we do something else while an employee is talking to us, the employee perceives we are not listening. Employees equate listening with our perception of their value. If we listen, we value them. If it appears we are not listening, we do not value them. So, they stop talking to us.

The key to listening well is to stop doing anything else. Stop talking. Stop typing. Stop reading email. Cut off distractions and look at the person. Let them talk (within reason). Ask questions. If you can master only one communication process, listening is the one.

First-line supervisors rarely have to be polished presenters—most of their verbal communication is one-on-one or more informal, small group meetings. Employees are not concerned with how articulate and glib you are. They want honesty, sincerity, and clarity. If you can do those three things, you're a communications star.

For many supervisors, a new and intimidating type of communication is writing. There are many jobs in which the ability to write clearly and concisely is not very important. However, as a supervisor, writing reports, disciplinary actions, email and performance appraisals can be fraught with problems.

If you aren't a good speller or have the best grammar, it's time to work on it. Your written communication has a lot to do with your credibility, especially up the chain. While you're working on improving this area, find someone to edit your work. There's nothing wrong with recognizing a weakness and taking the actions needed to mitigate the shortcoming.

Let's talk email for a minute. Email is great. I can send information to a lot of people at one time. We all don't have to be at the same place. We can even work different schedules, and everyone still gets the information. Email is fast and easy.

All of the characteristics that make email a great tool make email a trap. It is very easy to write an email in the heat of the moment and send it before we have a chance to engage our brain.

Once we send an email, we have lost control. Any of the people we sent it to can send it to anyone else.

Email is as much a permanent record as any other correspondence. Deleted email is not gone. It is common practice for courts to subpoena email correspondence and to require companies to produce email that may have been deleted.

My rules for email:

- Make the same effort on your email as you do for any other correspondence. Professional wording, grammar and spelling matter.
- Never talk about an employee (or boss) in an email.
- Write for the jury. Pretend every email you write could end up read on television, printed in the paper, or provided to a jury.
- Send email only to people who need it.

Some of the issues in communication that are common with new supervisors are due to how we think, more than our abilities in communicating.

By the time many people become supervisors, they have been in the workforce for some time. They have gained experience about the expectations of the workplace in general and about the expectations of their workplace specifically. A fundamental barrier to communication is the "everybody knows" syndrome.

We assume that because we know, everyone else should know.

I don't need to tell my employees they need to be on time, because "everybody knows" you have to be on time for work. I don't have to tell someone that their dress is not appropriate because "everybody knows" what the correct dress is in our workplace.

Many of us cannot remember that we didn't know either until someone told us. This is often one of the barriers to being clear about expectations and priorities. We assume the people who work for us have the same knowledge and experience.

The next mindset that needs to change is the, "I shouldn't have to tell someone more than once" syndrome. Yes, you do.

If you study marketing, you'll hear the adage that a consumer has to be exposed to a message at least 7 times before it sticks—preferably more. Just like us, employees have a lot of messages bombarding them and their brain filters out the majority of those, especially if they don't particularly like the message.

Repetition is necessary. But…once you can see your employees' lips moving at the same time you are talking, you can probably repeat yourself less often.

Put Your Knowledge to Work

Choose an area of communication that is difficult for you. Focus on that area, practice and ask for feedback to help you improve.

Key Takeaway

Communication is critical but can be difficult. Even the best communicator gets it wrong sometimes.

Chapter 16

Collaboration and Teamwork

"Talent wins games, but teamwork and intelligence win championships."
~ Michael Jordan

- Do your employees work together or does it seem like they are pulling in different directions?
- If you need help from another section, do you feel comfortable you'll get it?
- If one person gets behind, do others offer to help?
- Do you ever hear, "That's not my job?"

Frequently, at the front-line worker level, one can get away with being a lone wolf. However, that doesn't work well once a person moves into a supervisory role. Collaboration is vital. Not only do supervisors need to work well with their own people, they need to work well with others throughout the organization, which requires a broader view of the organization and our role within it.

I originally lumped collaboration-related skills into the other areas, but over time, I have come to the realization this is an important skill that needs to be emphasized. Collaboration includes things like:

- Being able to see the big picture
- Building and maintaining relationships
- Teamwork

Just because we can communicate well with individuals doesn't mean we can build a network of interlocking people in order to get things done.

Seeing the Big Picture

Supervisors need to be able to see the bigger picture of how all departments need to work together to get things done for our customers. Companies do not spend money on departments and people they do not think are necessary, so whether we can see their value or not, those with the ability to decide on the allocation of resources apparently do, so we need to figure it out.

Everyone contributes to providing goods and services to our customers. Everyone.

What do I need from other departments that would make my work life easier? What do they need from me?

I generally find that most of the time, everyone needs clear, timely information. If I get that, I can do my job better. If I can give that to others, they tend to be more willing to help me.

Building and Maintaining Relationships

Many supervisors don't work well with people they do not like, whether that person works for them or is a manager in another department. It is vital that a supervisor learns that liking isn't necessary—collaboration is.

Even with people we know and like, effort to build and maintain good relationships greases the wheels of cooperation in the workplace.

Supervisors should have a grasp of Networking 101 principles and how those principles translate into making their job easier.

Rule number 1: Give before you get. People are more willing to help others when they know they can also get help when needed. Don't always be the needy one.

Rule number 2: Everyone likes to be appreciated. Every department plays a role in the company's success. Acknowledging someone else's contribution doesn't diminish yours.

Establishing good relationships with other department managers can help make your job easier. The same goes with relationships with vendors and even regulatory agencies.

Calling a Group a Team Doesn't Make It So

I cannot tell you how many times employees have told me, "Management thinks if they call us a team, we'll be one. Just because they use the word, 'team' doesn't make it so."

Amen.

Although companies have put a lot of emphasis on the concept of teamwork, they do not do a good job of teaching people to work in teams.

A group of people working in the same area does not constitute a team. A group of people working together on their work is a work group, not a team.

The issue here is that Americans are taught to work alone. All through school, we hear, "Do your own work." We are graded on what we did—collaboration is cheating.

But somehow, once we are in the workplace, we are expected to know how to work as a part of a team.

A team is special. A definition is "a diverse group of people with complementary skills who are working together toward a common goal for which they hold one another accountable."

The important things in our team definition are "diverse", "complementary skills", "common goal" and "hold one another accountable."

We tend to hire people like ourselves, which dilutes the power of the team. Yes, people who think differently, talk differently or act differently, can make it more difficult to communicate and can increase conflict. But we can also come up with new and innovative ideas.

We think of diversity based upon race and sex, but differences in experience, education and personality are also important.

Complementary skills also require people who are not the same as us. I need people different than me to balance the team. I am very good at some things but have some significant deficiencies. Fortunately, I know what those are, and I hire people for my team who are very good at the things I am not.

Some people have specific skills at facilitating group work. They are valuable for that reason alone. Look for them and take advantage of that talent.

Having a clear common goal will go a long way toward channeling conflict into positive channels versus negative ones. We are all working toward the same thing. That becomes the overriding concern for the team.

Teams hold one another accountable. Everyone doesn't have to come to me to get someone to do his/her job. The members of the team can handle that themselves. They can set expectations and give feedback when expectations aren't met. If I demonstrate appropriate behaviors to communicate expectations and feedback, my employees will pick up those behaviors as well.

Put Your Knowledge to Work

Sit down and think about all of the departments you interact with. Why are they important? What can they do for you? How could you make their job easier? Don't know? Ask.

Have another supervisor that you have trouble working with? Is it a matter of personality or is there some conflict between the departments? If it is personality, learn to live with it. If there's a conflict, address it and work it out.

Are all of your employees like you? Do you value differences? Think through the role each person plays as a member of your team. Are there gaps that inhibit performance? If so, try to fill that gap with your next hire.

Key Takeaway

Relationships matter. Invest in building and nurturing relationships to help make processes work more smoothly.

Chapter 17

Conflict

"Peace is not the absence of conflict, it is the ability to handle conflict by peaceful means." ~ Ronald Reagan

- When you hear the expression, "workplace conflict," what comes to mind?
- What emotions do you feel when you find yourself in a conflict with a coworker? Your boss? A subordinate?
- How do you react to conflict?
- Do you ever think to yourself, "Why can't everyone just get along?"

Conflict is basically a difference between two people. We have different ideas, different priorities, different values, and different goals. In and of itself, it is not entirely good nor entirely bad.

It is how conflict is handled that makes a difference.

One of the greatest areas of supervisor fears is handling conflict. Most are averse to conflict.

In fact, we might argue that someone who enjoys conflict may not be the appropriate person for a supervisor role, although for different reasons than those who avoid conflict. This is another area where mindset is the fundamental problem.

Many people assume if there is conflict, it is a bad thing. And yes, oftentimes that is true.

Conflict can indeed, be a drain on productivity and lead to all sorts of problems, most of which fall upon the supervisor to deal with.

However, conflict is also the basis for problem solving and creativity. If there was no conflict, there would be no change, no improvement.

My husband and I have been married for 38 years. He is the love of my life, but that certainly doesn't mean we always see eye to eye. It does mean we have to have ways to ensure the conflict doesn't harm our relationship.

It's the same thing in the workplace. If you have two people, there will be conflict. It is normal.

The supervisor's job is to manage the conflict so that it remains a positive element, instead of escalating into World War III.

So what tips can I share?

First of all, model good conflict management skills. People do what they see. If you don't have the skills, learn them.

I lay out some specific techniques and when to use them in the Supervisor Academy course on Conflict Management. However, there are usually training seminars on this topic in most communities; attend one.

Next, remember that not every conflict has to be resolved. If the conflict is minor and is not interfering with getting the work done, why do you have to get involved with it?

It's not your problem. Ignore it. It may not go away, but it's not important. But if it affects work getting done, that's a different story.

You'll save yourself headaches if you teach your people how to resolve most conflicts on their own. Most disagreements can be worked out.

The secret is to have an overriding perspective about what's important. If I can keep people focused on the end goal, they can use that as the yardstick to measure different options and figure out the best approach. They're adults. Treat them like it.

Be prepared to invest time on issues of high importance. You may need help.

Your HR department should have someone with facilitation or mediation skills. Ask for help. There's no shame in that. Sometimes we are just too close to the issue to deal with it effectively. If you don't have someone with that skill set, you may have to go outside the organization.

Lastly, do not permit bullying behavior. Ever.

If you have a bully, you may not be aware of conflict, but it is there, bubbling beneath the surface. It stifles new ideas and creates stress—leading to absenteeism and poor morale. If you can't retrain the bully (and it is sometimes possible), then get rid of them. Sooner than later.

A moderate level of conflict can be a great thing. Disagreements about different approaches to a problem can lead to a better solution.

Encourage people to ask questions, to disagree, and to voice different points of view. Praise people for speaking up.

Put Your Knowledge to Work

Keep a conflict journal for a month or two. After you are involved in a conflict, write down the circumstances. Who did what. Who said what. After the emotion has dissipated, think through what happened. What did I say or do that seemed to help get a positive result? What did I say or do that seemed to make things worse? Why? What might I have said or done differently to reach a better outcome?

The purpose is to retrain our minds, so we react more appropriately the next time we are in a similar situation.

Key Takeaway

Conflict is normal. We need to encourage positive conflict in the workplace.

Your employees learn the appropriate way to deal with conflict from you. Model the behaviors you want to see, and you will see a dramatic difference in how conflict is handled by the people who work for you.

Chapter 18

Change

"If you always do what you've always done, you'll always get what you've always got." ~ Henry Ford

- What was the last organizational change announced in your organization?
- Did it succeed? Why/why not?

Supervisors are vital to any change effort. But most are not prepared for the ways they can help their employees accept and implement change in the workplace.

Most managers seem to believe that just announcing a change is enough to make it happen. Not so.

It is no wonder most organizational change efforts fail. It is easy enough to buy new facilities or equipment. It is not hard to redesign processes. The difficult piece is getting the support of the people who have to operate the equipment or to use the new process.

People make change work. Or not. I have seen people make even a bad process work. And I have seen them sabotage something that could have been a positive game-changer for their organization.

In most cases, they didn't set out to sabotage the change; they just didn't get behind it. I don't fault the people. I fault the organization.

Supervisors are in a key location to communicate the change and to enlist support. Often when rolling out a change, organizations do not sell the first-line supervisors. Management just announces the change.

Supervisors don't really get much information about why the change is happening, so we tell our people, "Just do it." Hardly a good sales pitch. Your support, and subsequently, the support of the people who work for you, is a necessary part of making change work.

Employees sometimes believe management stays up nights thinking of things to change just to put their mark on the organization.

That seems cynical to management perhaps, but it isn't always a wrong assumption. Employees have been through announced changes time after time.

As one employee told me, "I'm not doing anything for at least a few months. Management announces these changes all the time, but they can't stay focused. They'll be all over this for a few weeks and then they'll forget about it. Why put a lot of effort into something they are going to lose interest in a month or two from now?"

Good question.

Change is scary. It is made more so when management doesn't feel the need to explain the reasons they decided on the change.

As one CEO said to me, "Employees don't ask questions. I tell them what to do and they do it. That's all they need to know."

You can guess where he is (not) now.

What is going to be different after the change? Why is making the change important? Most importantly, "How is this change going to affect me?"

If we can't answer these questions, we shouldn't be making the change, because we apparently haven't thought it through.

But you need to make a change.

As a supervisor, ask questions. What is the problem we're solving? What positive outcome are we looking for? Then think about how the change is going to affect your department and your employees. Focus on the outcome desired. As much as possible, try to give your people as much input as possible into the how. Our people know the work. Take advantage of their expertise. Having some control over the change will make the change more palatable. You'll hear this referred to as gaining buy-in.

What if you have someone who just refuses to change? Usually there is a reason. Most people are not just going to refuse to change for no reason whatsoever. Talk to the person to discover what their issue is with the change. They may not understand. They may be concerned with their job security or working relationships. They may truly think it is a bad idea. Ask why. They may know something management didn't, or they may have a better way.

Or they could be a dinosaur who just doesn't want to change. Remind them dinosaurs are extinct. That should be a last resort, but sometimes that is the only answer left.

Usually, change involves changing habits. Habits are comfortable. We can work faster because we know what to do and how to do it. Now I have to be conscious and careful to do things differently. It takes some time to change habits.

If we stop paying attention too soon, people will fall back into their comfortable work habits. At some point, the change will become habit. We just have to pay attention until then.

Put Your Knowledge to Work

The next time you want to implement a change, think through the people piece. Be prepared to answer the questions and follow all the way through until the new habit is ingrained.

Better yet, tell your people what problem you want to solve and let them come up with the solution. Win-win!

Key Takeaway

Change is hard and often scary. Make it easier.

Chapter 19

Hire Right!

"You're only as good as the people you hire." ~ Ray Kroc

- How successful are your hires? Do they stay? Why do they leave or why do you let them go?
- What is the hiring process at your company? Do you understand it?

According to the Pareto Principle, 80% of the productivity in your workplace is due to 20% of the people. On the flip side, 80% of your problems come from 20% of your people. My experience has been it's more like 80% of my problems come from 5% of my people.

If we could just hire the right people to start with, we could solve most of our people problems.

The problem is there is no 100% certain way to hire the right person every time. If there was, I would be disgustingly wealthy.

Just because I can't be 100% perfect doesn't mean I can't do better. So can you. If you can get the opportunity to get training on better hiring, take it.

Hiring truth number 1: Hire in haste; repent at leisure. Most of us put off hiring until the pain level is higher than the pain level of the hiring process. Consequently, we're in a hurry and are more likely to settle for less than we want.

Take your time. If you just need a warm, breathing body for now, call a temporary staffing agency and fill the space until you can find the right person.

Hiring truth number 2: We hire for technical skills and fire for soft skills. We assess technical skills during the hiring process because that is relatively easy. We tend to ignore soft skills, like playing well with others, because that's harder to evaluate. But those are the very skills that cause us to decide to let someone go. So we have to figure out how to evaluate those soft skills that are important in our organization.

To do a better job, use a process to be sure you have the best information possible when deciding who to hire. Use your HR department if you have one. They really are there to help you. But you have to talk to them. The better they understand what you do, the better they can help you sort out the best possible candidates. Use them.

In most organizations, supervisors have the authority to hire. Use that authority well. Because we are in a hurry, the tendency is to skip steps—especially things like background checks.

Our tendency is to hire people like us. We feel comfortable with people who look like, talk like, and act like us. We are not benefitted by a bunch of mini-me's. Instead, know what the job requires, determine priorities and measure the knowledge and skills of the people you interview against those requirements, not your personal reactions to the person.

Interviews are notoriously inaccurate in determining the best-qualified person. I don't advocate doing away with interviews altogether, but don't give them too much weight in the decision process. You can improve the success of interviewing by getting training in this area. There are a lot of potential legal issues in the hiring in addition to finding the right person. Training on hiring and on interviewing can keep you out of trouble and improve your ability to make a good hire.

Supervisors often act like people would be lucky to work for them. Consequently, they do not treat potential employees as important.

Remember the hiring process is a two-way process. You're deciding whether you want to hire a person. They are deciding whether they want to work for you. With the unemployment rate at its current levels, candidates have options.

Put Your Knowledge to Work

Think about people you hired who didn't work out. Why did you have to let them go (or why did they choose to leave?) Is there anything you could have done during the hiring process that could have helped you avoid this hire?

Key Takeaway

Hiring the right person can prevent a lot of headaches. Hire in haste; repent at leisure. Take time to do it right.

Summary

Supervising others is challenging and rewarding. Some days it is frustrating. Other days you're riding high.

The first-line supervisor is critical to an organization's success—whether company leadership knows it or not.

None of us are perfect supervisors. We can all be better. Being a supervisor carries the responsibility to achieve results, develop our people, continuously learn, and look for opportunities to change things for the better. A big responsibility.

Develop a network of other supervisors as your support team. You'll need them, and they'll need you as well.

Good luck!

Want to Know More?

Finding resources designed for first-line supervisors can be tough. It is difficult to let supervisors go for extended periods for training. Here are two additional resources that may be helpful in your supervisory development program.

Winning the War for Profit: Developing Leaders Where It Really Matters. (2017) Written for organizational leaders, this book shows why they need to focus on developing leaders at the bottom of the leadership ladder and provides a step-by-step process to select, train and support first-line supervisors.

The Supervisor Academy. Developed by the author, The Supervisor Academy (https://supervisor-academy/thinkific.com) is a series of short (approximately 1 hour), on-line tutorials on a variety of supervisory subjects. Works well alone or in conjunction with *Leadership in the Trenches: Developing First-line Leaders*. Email thesupervisoracademy@gmail.com and mention this book to receive a code for one free online course.

ABOUT THE AUTHOR

Penny Miller spent 21 years in the United States Air Force, working in the human resources arena. Her last assignment was as a squadron commander, overseeing human resources for a large installation. It was in the armed forces that she developed a deep appreciation for the first-line supervisory role and its importance in organizational excellence. That passion stayed with her in corporate HR.

In 2007, she founded Venture HRO, later renamed My HR Department, an HR consulting company. Most of her practice centers around training and coaching organizational leaders, with her primary focus on those leading "in the trenches," where the War for Profit is waged.

www.ingramcontent.com/pod-product-compliance
Lightning Source LLC
Chambersburg PA
CBHW071409220526
45469CB00004B/1214